SANJEEV KAPOOR

Vegetarian

FINGER FOODS

In association with Alyona Kapoor

Popular Prakashan
www.popularprakashan.com

Published by
POPULAR PRAKASHAN PVT. LTD.
301, Mahalaxmi Chambers
22, Bhulabhai Desai Road
Mumbai - 400 026
for KHANA KHAZANA PUBLICATIONS PVT. LTD.

First Published 2014

(4376)
ISBN: 978-81-7991-817-3

Design: Anjali Sawant
Photography: Alim Bolar, Bharat Bhirangi & Mukesh Munim

PRINTED IN INDIA
by Sai Print 'O' Pack
New Delhi - 110 020

Author's Note

Finger foods are small pieces of tasty food that most of us love to nibble and indulge in more than any other kinds of meals. *Vegetarian Finger Foods* is replete with recipes that are *chatpatta*, easy to make, look good on the table and can be used any time while entertaining. What is more, many of these delectable bite-sized foods can be made from leftovers from a previous meal. Try out Biscuit Puri, Honey Potato Fingers, Corn and Vegetable Lollipops and many many more such recipes and get your family and friends to eat from your fingers, literally. Try the recipes that are detailed and perfected over the years or try a variation.

The Stuffed Mushrooms, Green Pea Potli, Fried Idli with Sichuan Sauce, Til Moongphali Aloo and Dilli Aloo Tikki Chaat in this book are some of my favourites. Try them any time and you'll never go wrong.

Happy Cooking!

Contents

Bhakarwadi

Ingredients

1 cup refined flour

¾ cup gram flour

Salt to taste

¼ teaspoon turmeric powder

1 teaspoon red chilli powder

1 tablespoon oil + for deep-frying

Filling

¼ cup poppy seeds

¼ cup sesame seeds

½ cup grated dried coconut

1 tablespoon fresh ginger, finely chopped

3 green chillies, finely chopped

½ tablespoon coriander powder

½ tablespoon cumin powder

2 teaspoons red chilli powder

½ teaspoon turmeric powder

¼ teaspoon asafoetida

2 tablespoons fresh coriander, finely chopped

Salt to taste

Method

1. Mix together the refined flour, gram flour and salt in a bowl. Add the turmeric powder, chilli powder and one tablespoon of oil. Add enough water to make a stiff dough. Cover with a damp cloth and set aside.
2. For the filling, dry-roast the poppy seeds, sesame seeds and coconut separately.
3. In another bowl, mix the chopped ginger, green chillies, coriander powder, cumin powder, chilli powder and turmeric powder.
4. Add the roasted spices and mix well. Add the asafoetida, chopped coriander and salt; mix well and divide into eight equal portions.
5. Divide the dough into eight equal portions. Roll out each portion into a thin round. Apply a little water on the surface and spread one portion of the filling. Roll into a cylinder.
6. Place the rolls in a steamer and steam for twenty minutes.
7. Cool the rolls slightly and cut into half-inch pieces. The rolls can also be cut into pieces without steaming.
8. Heat the oil in a non-stick *kadai* and deep-fry the *bhakharwadi* over a medium heat till golden brown and crisp. Drain on absorbent paper. Serve hot or cold.

Chilli Cheese Toast

Ingredients

8 slices of bread

1½ cups grated cheese

4-6 green chillies, finely chopped

½ medium bunch fresh coriander, chopped

1 medium onion, chopped

1 medium capsicum (optional), chopped

1 teaspoon crushed peppercorns

Salt to taste

Method

1. In a bowl, mix the cheese, green chillies, coriander leaves, onion, capsicum, crushed peppercorns and salt. Divide the mixture into eight equal portions.
2. Heat a non-stick *tawa* and toast the bread slices on one side. Apply the cheese mixture on the non-toasted side of the bread slices.
3. Preheated the oven to 180°C/350°F/Gas Mark 4. Grill the toast in the preheated oven until the cheese melts and turns golden brown. Cut each slice diagonally into two and serve hot with a sauce of your choice.

Sandwich Dhokla

Ingredients

1 cup rice
¼ cup split skinless black gram
¼ cup skimmed milk sour yogurt
Salt to taste
2 teaspoons ginger paste
1½ teaspoons green chilli paste
½ teaspoon soda bicarbonate
1 tablespoon lemon juice
½ cup thick Green Chutney (page 12)
2 tablespoons chopped fresh coriander

Method

1. Dry-roast the rice and the gram over a medium heat for four to five minutes. Cool and grind into a moderately coarse powder.
2. Put the powder into a bowl. Add the yogurt and one and a half cups of warm water. Mix thoroughly to make a smooth batter of pouring consistency. Stir in the salt.
3. Leave the batter to ferment for eight to ten hours.

4. Add the ginger paste and green chilli paste to the batter and mix well.
5. Boil some water in a pressure cooker.
6. Pour half the batter in a separate bowl. In a small bowl, mix one-fourth teaspoon of soda bicarbonate and half a tablespoon of lemon juice. Add to the batter and whisk well. Repeat this procedure for the remaining batter just before putting it into the steamer.
7. Pour the batter into a *thali* and place it in the pressure cooker. Steam without the weight for eight to ten minutes. Test for doneness with a knife. If the knife comes out clean, it is cooked. Remove from the cooker and spread green chutney over the *dhokla* while hot.
8. Pour the remaining batter over the chutney and steam again for ten minutes. Remove from the cooker, cool slightly, and garnish with chopped coriander.
9. Cut into desired shapes and serve hot.

GREEN CHUTNEY

Grind together 1 cup fresh coriander, ½ cup fresh mint, 2-3 green chillies, black salt to taste, ¼ teaspoon sugar and 1 tablespoon lemon juice to a smooth paste using a little water if required.

Spinach And Cheese Idli

Ingredients

8-10 spinach leaves
¼ cup grated cheese
½ cup split skinless black gram
1 cup *idli rawa*
Salt to taste
½ teaspoon crushed black peppercorns

Method

1. Soak the *urad dal* and *idli rawa* separately for three to four hours.
2. Drain and grind the *dal*, sprinkling water as required, to make a smooth, spongy batter.
3. Drain the *idli rawa* and add it with the salt to the *dal* batter and mix thoroughly with your hands, using a whipping motion so that the batter is mixed well.
4. Place the batter in a large non-stick pan or bowl, cover tightly and rest in a warm place for twenty-four hours, or at least overnight.
5. Blanch the spinach leaves in boiling water for two to three minutes. Reserve a few leaves and purée the rest. Shred the reserved leaves.

6. Add the spinach purée to the *idli* batter and mix well. Pour into lightly-oiled *idli* moulds, top with the shredded spinach leaves and grated cheese.
7. Sprinkle crushed peppercorns and steam till the *idli* are done.
8. Serve the *idli* with chilli sauce or chilli garlic sauce.

Fried Idli With Sichuan Sauce

Ingredients

10-12 *idli*, cut into fingers
2 tablespoons oil + for deep-frying
6 garlic cloves, chopped
4 spring onions, sliced
2 tablespoons Sichuan Sauce (page 15)
2 tablespoons tomato ketchup
3 stalks spring onion greens, sliced

Method

1. Heat sufficient oil in a non-stick *kadai* and deep-fry the *idli* fingers till golden and crisp. Drain on absorbent paper.
2. Heat two tablespoons of oil in a non-stick *kadai*; add the garlic and sauté for half a minute. Add the spring onions and continue to sauté for another minute.
3. Add the Sichuan sauce and tomato ketchup and stir to mix. Add the fried *idli* and sauté over a medium heat for one minute, tossing and stirring continuously.
4. Add the spring onion greens and toss again to mix well. Serve hot.

SICHUAN SAUCE

Boil 10-12 dried red chillies in 1 cup of water for 5 to 7 minutes. Drain, cool and grind to a fine paste. Heat ½ cup oil in a pan; add 10 finely chopped garlic cloves, 2 finely chopped green chillies, 2 finely chopped spring onions and 1 inch ginger, grated, and sauté for 1 minute. Add the red chilli paste and sauté for a few more seconds. Add 2-3 inches celery stalk, finely chopped, 3 tablespoons tomato ketchup and salt to taste, and stir well to mix. Stir in 2 teaspoons white vinegar and simmer for 1 minute till the oil rises to the surface. Cool and store.

Note: Sichuan sauce will keep for 1 month if there is sufficient oil covering the surface.

Achari Idli

Ingredients

35-40 mini *idli*
2 tablespoons refined mustard oil
4 dried red chillies
½ teaspoon mustard seeds
¼ teaspoon fenugreek seeds
¾ teaspoon cumin seeds
½ teaspoon fennel seeds
½ teaspoon onion seeds
Salt to taste
2 tablespoons chopped fresh coriander

Method

1. Heat the mustard oil to smoking point and set aside to cool.
2. Dry-roast the red chillies, mustard seeds, fenugreek seeds, cumin seeds, fennel seeds and onion seeds till fragrant. Grind to a powder, add the salt and mix with the cooled oil.
3. Place the ground spices mixture in a non-stick pan and heat gently. Add the *idli* and toss well to mix. Serve hot, garnished with the chopped coriander.

Chef's Tip: If mini *idli* are not available, you can cut regular *idli* into quarters for this recipe.

Vegetable Idli

Ingredients

1 cup parboiled rice

½ cup split black gram

Salt to taste

1 medium-sized carrot, grated

4-5 French beans, chopped

2-3 cauliflower florets, grated

½ medium-sized green capsicum, chopped

1 inch ginger

2 tablespoons oil

15-20 black peppercorns, crushed

2 tablespoons chopped fresh coriander

Method

1. Soak the rice and *dal* separately for at least four hours. Drain and grind the rice with some water to a coarse batter; grind the *dal* with water to a thin batter.
2. Mix both the batters together, adding water if necessary, to make a batter of dropping consistency.

3. Add the salt, cover and leave to ferment overnight or for four or five hours, in a warm place.
4. Add the vegetables to the fermented batter and mix well.
5. Lightly grease the *idli* moulds with oil. Pour a spoonful of batter into each mould. Sprinkle each *idli* with crushed peppercorns and chopped coriander.
6. Heat some water in a pressure cooker and place the *idli* stand in it. Seal the cooker with the lid and steam without the weight for ten minutes, or till done.
7. Serve hot with chutney.

Grilled Corn And Capsicum Toasties

Ingredients

8 slices white bread
1 cup sweet corn kernels, boiled
1 medium green capsicum, chopped
1½ cups grated cheese
2-3 green chillies, chopped
2 tablespoons chopped fresh coriander
1 medium onion, chopped
7-8 black peppercorns, crushed
Salt to taste

Method

1. Preheat oven to 180°C/350°F/Gas Mark 4.
2. In a bowl, mix the sweet corn, capsicum, cheese, green chillies, chopped coriander, onion, crushed peppercorns and salt. Divide the mixture into eight equal portions.
3. Toast the slices of bread on one side on a non-stick *tawa*. Spread the corn and cheese mixture on the other side. Place on a baking tray and bake till the topping turns golden brown. Cut each slice diagonally in half and serve hot with tomato ketchup.

Corn And Vegetable Lollipops

Ingredients

½ cup fresh corn kernels, crushed
1 medium carrot, finely chopped
¼ cup shelled green peas, crushed
2 large potatoes, boiled and mashed
16 baby corn cobs
1 tablespoon oil + for deep-frying
Salt to taste
1 inch piece fresh ginger, chopped
4-6 cloves garlic, peeled and chopped
2-3 green chillies, chopped
1 medium onion, peeled and chopped
1 tablespoon chopped fresh coriander
½ tablespoon light soy sauce
½ teaspoon white pepper powder
¼ teaspoon MSG (optional)
2 tablespoons cornflour
¼ cup refined flour

Method

1. Heat one tablespoon of oil in a non-stick pan. Add the carrot and peas and stir. Add the crushed corn and salt, and cook till the vegetables soften slightly.

2. Place the mashed potatoes in a bowl; add the sautéed vegetables, ginger, garlic, green chillies, chopped onion and coriander, soy sauce, white pepper powder, MSG, salt and cornflour. Mix thoroughly.

3. Divide the mixture into sixteen equal portions. Roll each portion into a smooth ball and insert the thicker end of a baby corn into the ball. Press the mixture lightly between your palms to secure the baby corn.

4. Heat sufficient oil in a non-stick wok; roll the prepared lollipops in flour, shake to remove excess flour and deep-fry for three to four minutes over a medium heat, or till crisp and golden brown, turning occasionally.

5. Drain on absorbent paper. Serve hot with Sichuan Sauce (page 15).

Corn Handvo

Ingredients

1 cup crushed sweet corn kernels
1 cup rice
½ cup split pigeon peas
¼ cup split skinless green gram
2 tablespoons split Bengal gram
2 tablespoons split skinless black gram
½ cup sour yogurt
2 teaspoons soda bicarbonate
Salt to taste
4 teaspoons sugar
2 teaspoons red chilli powder
½ teaspoon turmeric powder
1 medium carrot, grated
½ cup shelled green peas, boiled
5 tablespoons oil
2 dried red chillies
2 cloves
1 bay leaf
A pinch of asafoetida
2 teaspoons mustard seeds
1 tablespoon lemon juice
3 tablespoons toasted sesame seeds

Method

1. Soak the rice with all the dal in five cups of water for two hours. Drain.
2. Grind the rice to a coarse paste and add enough water to make a batter of medium consistency. Mix in the yogurt and one teaspoon of soda bicarbonate. Cover the batter and leave to stand in a dark place for two or three hours to ferment.
3. Stir in the corn, salt, sugar, chilli powder and turmeric powder into the batter. Mix in the grated carrot and green peas.
4. Heat the oil in a pan; add the red chillies, cloves, bay leaf, asafoetida and mustard seeds and sauté till the seeds begin to splutter.
5. Sprinkle the remaining soda bicarbonate over the batter and pour the lemon juice into it. Immediately pour the hot spices into the batter and whisk briskly.
6. Grease a ring mould. Pour the batter into it till half full. Sprinkle the toasted sesame seeds generously over the top.
7. Place about two kilograms of clean sand in a large pressure cooker.
8. Place the ring mould in the sand carefully, pressing down till it is embedded about half way into the sand. Cover the cooker with the lid but without the gasket and whistle.

9. Place over a high heat for ten minutes. Lower the heat to medium and cook the *handvo* till a skewer inserted into it comes out clean. It may take forty to forty-five minutes.

10. Cool slightly and unmould the *handvo*. Cut into thick slices and serve hot with Green Chutney (page 12).

Sesame Corn Toast

Ingredients

½ cup toasted sesame seeds

1 cup fresh corn kernels, finely minced

8 slices bread

3 medium potatoes

1 medium green capsicum, seeded and finely chopped

1 medium onion, finely chopped

1 inch ginger, peeled and finely chopped

4-6 garlic cloves, peeled and finely chopped

2-3 green chillies, seeded and finely chopped

2 tablespoons fresh coriander, finely chopped

½ tablespoon soy sauce

½ cup cornflour

½ teaspoon white pepper powder

¼ teaspoon MSG (optional)

Salt to taste

Oil for deep-frying

Method

1. Boil the potatoes. Cool, peel and mash them in a deep bowl.
2. Add the minced corn, chopped capsicum, onion, ginger, garlic, green chillies, coriander, soy sauce, two tablespoons of cornflour, white pepper powder, MSG and salt. Mix thoroughly.
3. Mix the remaining cornflour with half a cup of water. Cut the slices of bread with a round cookie cutter into one-inch circles.
4. Brush the circles with the cornflour mixture and spread a thick layer of the corn mixture, smoothening it with wet fingers. Sprinkle sesame seeds generously and press lightly. Shake off the excess seeds and refrigerate for fifteen minutes.
5. Heat sufficient oil in a non-stick wok and deep-fry the sesame-corn-bread rounds for two to three minutes, or until crisp and golden brown, turning occasionally.
6. Drain on absorbent paper. Serve hot with a sauce of your choice.

Falafel

Ingredients

1 cup chickpeas
2-3 garlic cloves, peeled and chopped
A few sprigs of fresh coriander, chopped
A few sprigs of fresh parsley, chopped
4-5 stalks spring onion greens, chopped
¼ cup breadcrumbs
A small pinch of soda bicarbonate
½ teaspoon cumin powder
Salt to taste
¼ teaspoon black pepper powder
½ teaspoon paprika
Oil for deep-frying

Method

1. Wash and soak chickpeas overnight or for at least 6 hours. Drain and spread on a kitchen towel to dry.
2. Grind the chickpeas with the chopped garlic, coriander, parsley, spring onion greens and breadcrumbs coarsely.

3. Add the soda bicarbonate and the cumin powder and mix well.
4. Season with salt, pepper and paprika. Knead the mixture well and leave to rest for a couple of hours in a refrigerator.
5. Shape the mixture with the help of two damp tablespoons, scooping the mixture from one tablespoon to the other till you get a uniform oval shape. Make all the falafels and store on a greased plate in a refrigerator till ready to fry.
6. Heat oil in a non-stick *kadai* and deep-fry the falafels till golden brown. Drain on absorbent paper and serve hot.

Chef's Tip: Falafels go well with tabbouleh salad and tahina dip. Falafel is traditionally made with fava beans but you can use chickpeas instead.

Paneer Koliwada

Ingredients

300 grams cottage cheese (*paneer*)
½ cup gram flour
½ teaspoon cumin powder
2 teaspoons Kashmiri red chilli powder
Salt to taste
1 tablespoon ginger paste
1 tablespoon garlic paste
2 tablespoons yogurt
2 tablespoons lemon juice
Oil for deep-frying
½ teaspoon *chaat masala*

Method

1. Cut the *paneer* into three-inch by half-inch by half-inch pieces.
2. Mix together the gram flour, cumin powder, chilli powder, salt, ginger paste, garlic paste, yogurt, lemon juice and a little water if necessary, into a thick batter.
3. Marinate the *paneer* in the batter for half an hour. Heat oil in a non-stick *kadai* and deep-fry the *paneer* till crisp on the outside. Serve hot, sprinkled with *chaat masala*.

Chef's Tip: To make Paneer Koliwada extra crisp, add a tablespoon of cornflour to the batter.

Crunchy Paneer Pakora

Ingredients

250 grams cottage cheese

1 cup *boondi*

Oil for deep-frying

Garlic Chutney

8-10 garlic cloves

1 teaspoon oil

1 teaspoon red chilli powder

Salt to taste

Batter

1 cup gram flour

1½ inch ginger

5 garlic cloves

1 teaspoon red chilli powder

½ tsp turmeric powder

A pinch of soda bicarbonate

Salt to taste

Method

1. Wash and cut the cottage cheese into two-inch by half-inch by half-inch sized batons. Slit each baton into half, leaving one edge intact for filling.
2. Crush the *boondi* with your hand and keep aside.

3. To make garlic chutney, peel and roast garlic in one teaspoon of oil. Mix with chilli powder and salt and grind to a smooth paste.
4. To prepare the batter, peel and wash ginger and garlic and grind together to make a paste. Mix this paste with the gram flour, chilli powder, turmeric powder, soda bicarbonate and salt. Add sufficient water and whisk well to make a batter of a coating consistency. Rest the batter for about fifteen minutes.
5. Stuff garlic chutney into the slit of each cottage cheese baton.
6. Heat sufficient oil in a non-stick *kadai*, dip each baton of cottage cheese into the batter, roll in the crushed *boondi* and deep-fry over a medium heat till crisp and golden brown.
7. Serve hot with a chutney of your choice.

Crunchy Paneer

Ingredients

300 grams cottage cheese (*paneer*), cut into 1-inch cubes

¼ cup refined flour

1 tablespoon oil + for deep-frying

½ inch ginger, chopped

2 garlic cloves, chopped

¼ celery stalk, chopped

Salt to taste

5-6 black peppercorns, crushed

A small pinch of MSG (optional)

½ tablespoon dark soy sauce

½ teaspoon sugar

1 teaspoon vinegar

2 stalks spring onion greens, sliced

Batter

¾ cup cornflour

6 tablespoons refined flour

½ teaspoon baking powder

Salt to taste

Method

1. Dust the *paneer* cubes with refined flour. Mix all the ingredients for the batter together with three-fourth cup plus one and a half tablespoons of chilled water and whisk with a balloon whisk till smooth.
2. Heat oil in a non-stick wok. Dip *paneer* cubes in the batter and deep-fry till golden and crisp. Drain on absorbent paper.
3. Heat one tablespoon of oil in a non-stick wok; add the ginger and garlic and sauté over medium heat for half a minute.
4. Add the celery and continue to sauté for half a minute more.
5. Add the fried paneer, salt, crushed peppercorns, MSG, soy sauce, sugar and vinegar and cook over high heat for one minute, stirring and tossing continuously.
6. Serve hot, garnished with spring onion greens.

Kasoori Paneer Tikka

Ingredients

250 grams cottage cheese (*paneer*)

1 medium green capsicum

1 medium onion, peeled

1 medium tomato, seeded

1 cup yogurt

2 tablespoons Green Chutney (page 12)

1 teaspoon green chilli paste

1 teaspoon ginger paste

1 teaspoon garlic paste

¼ teaspoon turmeric powder

½ teaspoon carom seeds

1 teaspoon *garam masala* powder

1 teaspoon *chaat masala*

2 tablespoons dried fenugreek leaves, roasted and crushed

2 tablespoons roasted split Bengal gram powder

¼ cup fresh cream

Salt to taste

2 tablespoons mustard oil

2 tablespoons oil

2 tablespoons lemon juice

Method

1. Cut the *paneer*, capsicum, onion and tomato into one-and-a-half-inch pieces.
2. Mix together the yogurt, green chutney, green chilli paste, ginger paste, garlic paste, turmeric powder, carom seeds, *garam masala* powder, half a teaspoon of *chaat masala*, crushed *kasoori methi*, roasted split Bengal gram powder, fresh cream and salt in a bowl. Add the *paneer* cubes and marinate for about fifteen minutes.
3. Heat the mustard oil to smoking point and set aside to cool. When completely cold, stir the oil into the *paneer* cubes.
4. Soak a few wooden skewers in water for fifteen minutes.
5. Thread the capsicum, *paneer*, tomato and onion cubes one after the other onto the skewers.
6. Cook on an oiled grill or non-stick *tawa*, turning the skewers a few times so that the *tikka* cook on all sides.
7. Arrange the *tikka* on a plate, sprinkle with the remaining *chaat masala* and lemon juice and serve hot.

Paneer Tikka

Ingredients

250 grams cottage cheese (*paneer*), cut into 2-inch pieces

½ cup drained yogurt

Salt to taste

1 teaspoon red chilli powder

¼ teaspoon turmeric powder

½ teaspoon *garam masala* powder

½ teaspoon dried mango powder

½ teaspoon lemon juice

1 teaspoon ginger paste

1 teaspoon garlic paste

Oil for basting

½ teaspoon *chaat masala*

1 lemon, cut into wedges

Method

1. Make a marinade of the drained yogurt, salt, chilli powder, turmeric powder, *garam masala* powder, dried mango powder, lemon juice, ginger paste and garlic paste.
2. Mix well with the *paneer* and set aside for one hour, preferably in the refrigerator.
3. Preheat a combi-oven to 240ºC/475ºF/Gas Mark 9.
4. Arrange the *paneer* in a single layer in an ovenproof dish and brush with oil.
5. Cook for five minutes, basting with oil half-way through. Turn the *paneer* over and cook again for five minutes, basting with oil again half-way through.
6. Sprinkle *chaat masala* and serve hot with lemon wedges.

Lehsuni Tikki

Ingredients

6 medium potatoes

Salt to taste

1 medium onion, finely chopped

4-6 garlic cloves, finely chopped

¼ cup fresh coriander, finely chopped

¼ cup cottage cheese

6-8 cashew nuts

½ tablespoon red chilli powder

Oil to deep-fry

Method

1. Wash, boil, cool, peel and mash the potatoes thoroughly. Add salt and knead the mashed potatoes to make a smooth dough. Divide into ten to twelve equal portions.
2. Grate the cottage cheese. Crush the cashew nuts and mix with the chopped onion, garlic, fresh coriander, chilli powder, salt and grated cottage cheese.
3. Divide the mixture into ten to twelve equal portions. Stuff each portion of mashed potato with a portion of the cottage cheese mixture. Roll and shape into *tikki* of approximately two-inch diameter and half an inch thickness. Heat oil in a non-stick *kadai* and deep-fry the *tikki* till golden brown. Remove and drain on absorbent paper. Serve hot with tomato ketchup or mint chutney.

Chatpati Tikki

Ingredients

2 medium unripe green bananas
2 medium carrots, grated
1 medium onion, finely chopped
1 inch ginger, finely chopped
3-4 cloves garlic, finely chopped
3-4 green chillies, finely chopped
8-10 mint leaves, finely chopped
15-20 raisins, roughly chopped
6 seedless dates, roughly chopped
½ cup roasted peanuts without skin
1 teaspoon oil
½ teaspoon mustard seeds
½ teaspoon split skinless black gram
1 teaspoon red chilli powder
2 teaspoons *chaat masala* powder
Salt to taste
2 teaspoons lemon juice

Method

1. Boil the whole unripe bananas in sufficient water for fifteen to twenty minutes. Cool, peel and mash well.
2. Mix the dates with the raisins and divide into twelve equal portions.

3. Grind the roasted peanuts to a coarse powder. Heat the oil in a non-stick pan and add the mustard seeds, let them crackle and add the black gram. When the black gram turns brown, add the chopped onion, ginger, garlic and green chillies. Stir-fry for half a minute. Add the chilli powder, mix and quickly add the grated carrot.
4. Cook over a medium heat for 2-3 minutes. Sprinkle the chopped mint leaves, *chaat masala*, mix well and remove from heat. Cool and mix the cooked *masala* with the mashed banana. Add salt to taste, lemon juice and mix well.
5. Divide the mixture into twelve equal portions. Stuff a portion of the date and raisin mixture into each portion of banana mixture. Wet your palm and form this mixture into a *tikki* of not more than half inch thickness.
6. Coat the *tikki* with the coarse peanut powder, pressing them lightly between your palms. Heat a non-stick pan or *tawa* and place the peanut coated *tikki* on it. Cook over a medium heat till the crust is crisp and nicely browned. Make sure that the *tikki* are heated through.
7. Serve immediately with a tangy sauce of your choice.

Dilli Aloo Tikki Chaat

Ingredients

Potato pattice

4 large potatoes, boiled, peeled and grated

Salt to taste

Oil for shallow-frying

Filling

1 cup split skinless black gram, soaked and boiled

1 tablespoon fresh coriander leaves, finely chopped

2 green chillies, finely chopped

Black salt to taste

A pinch of asafoetida

½ inch piece ginger, peeled and finely chopped

½ teaspoon *chaat masala*

½ teaspoon red chilli powder

Topping (one portion)

½ cup, dried yellow peas, soaked and boiled

¼ cup yogurt

2 tablespoons Date and Tamarind Chutney (page 46)

½ tablespoon Green Chutney (page 12)

¼ teaspoon roasted cumin powder

A pinch of black salt

¼ teaspoon *chaat masala* powder

¼ teaspoon red chilli powder

A few *papdi*, crushed

Method

1. Place the potatoes in a bowl, add the salt and mix well.
2. In another bowl, mix together the boiled black gram, chopped coriander, green chillies, black salt, asafoetida, ginger, *chaat masala* and chilli powder.
3. Knead the grated potatoes. Grease the palms of your hands. Flatten a portion of mashed potato on your palm and place a little filling on it. Bring the edges of the potato together and shape into a thick, round *tikki*.
4. Heat oil in a non-stick *tawa*, and shallow-fry the *tikki*. When one side turns golden brown, turn over and fry the other side the same way.
5. To serve, place a *tikki* on a plate. Hollow out the centre and put some *matara* in it. Top with dollops of yogurt, date and tamarind chutney and green chutney. Sprinkle roasted cumin powder, black salt, *chaat masala* powder and chilli powder. Crush a few *papdi* and sprinkle on top. Serve immediately.

DATE AND TAMARIND CHUTNEY

Wash, stone and chop 15-20 dates. Dry-roast 2 teaspoons cumin seeds and ¼ teaspoon fennel seeds. Cool and grind to a powder. Cook the dates, 1 cup tamarind pulp, cumin and fennel powder, ½ cup jaggery, 2 teaspoons red chilli powder, 1 teaspoon dried ginger powder, black salt, salt and four cups of water till thick.

Honey Potato Fingers

Ingredients

4 large potatoes, peeled and cut into thin fingers

4 tablespoons honey

½ cup cornflour

2 tablespoons oil + for deep-frying

2 garlic cloves, peeled and crushed

2 tablespoons light soy sauce

2 tablespoons Hoisin sauce

2 tablespoons red chilli flakes

Salt to taste

1 teaspoon lemon juice

1 tablespoon toasted sesame seeds

Method

1. Mix two tablespoons of cornflour and one cup of water.
2. Heat sufficient oil in a non-stick wok or pan, dust the potato fingers with the remaining cornflour and deep-fry, turning frequently, for about four to five minutes. Drain on absorbent paper.

3. Heat two tablespoons of oil in a non-stick wok or pan, add the garlic and stir-fry for a few seconds. Stir in the light soy sauce, Hoisin sauce, red chilli flakes and salt to taste.
4. Add the fried potato fingers and stir in the cornflour mixture. Cook over a moderate to high heat for a minute, stirring continuously.
5. Reduce the heat and stir in the lemon juice and honey, mix well and cook over a moderate heat for a couple of minutes.
6. Serve hot sprinkled with toasted sesame seeds.

Crostini Al Parmigiano

Parmesan Cheese Toasts

Ingredients

1 loaf of French bread (baguette)

½ cup grated Parmesan cheese

1 cup grated mozzarella cheese

10 garlic cloves, chopped

10-12 black peppercorns, freshly ground

½ tablespoon mixed dried herbs

½ tablespoon red chilli flakes

2 tablespoons butter

Method

1. Mix the Parmesan cheese, mozzarella cheese and garlic in a bowl.
2. Season with ground peppercorns, dried herbs and chilli flakes.
3. Cut the baguette diagonally into half-inch thick slices and spread with butter.
4. Spread the cheese mixture evenly on each slice and place under a hot grill till the cheese melts.
5. Serve hot.

Biscuit Puri

Ingredients

2 cups fine semolina

Salt to taste

2 tablespoons oil + to deep-fry

1 cup grated fresh coconut

1 medium-sized bunch fresh chopped coriander

3-4 green chillies, chopped fine

½ cup gram flour

Method

1. Mix the semolina with the salt. Heat two tablespoons of oil and add to the semolina and mix gently. Add sufficient water and knead into a semi-soft dough. Cover with a damp cloth and let it stand for at least two hours.
2. For the filling, mix together the coconut, chopped coriander, green chillies, gram flour and salt.
3. Knead the dough again and divide into sixteen equal portions. Also divide the filling into sixteen equal portions.

4. Grease your palms, shape one portion of the dough into a *puri*. Place a portion of the filling in the centre and gather the edges and roll again into a ball. Dust a little flour and roll again into a *puri* of three-inch diameter.
5. Heat sufficient oil in a non-stick *kadai* and gently slide in the *puri* one at a time. Deep-fry over a medium heat till both sides are golden.
6. Drain on an absorbent paper and serve hot.

Chef's Tip: You can also use wholewheat flour instead of fine semolina to make the dough.

Kathiawadi Vada

Ingredients

1 cup wholewheat grain

1 cup rice

¼ cup split skinless black gram

¼ cup split skinless green gram

¼ cup split Bengal gram

Salt to taste

A pinch of soda bicarbonate

¼ cup yogurt

2 teaspoons oil + for deep-frying

2-3 green chillies, chopped

1 inch ginger, chopped

1 small bunch fresh coriander, finely chopped

½ teaspoon turmeric powder

½ teaspoon sugar

A pinch of asafoetida

Method

1. Grind the wheat, rice and both the gram to a coarse flour.
2. Add the salt, soda bicarbonate, yogurt, two teaspoons of oil and little warm water to the coarsely ground flour mixture and make a thick batter.

3. Cover with a cloth and keep it in a warm place to ferment for eight to ten hours.
4. Grind the chillies and the ginger together into a fine paste.
5. Add the ginger-green chilli paste, turmeric powder, sugar, chopped coriander and asafoetida to the fermented batter. Mix well.
6. Heat sufficient oil in a non-stick *kadai*. Drop a tablespoonful of batter into the hot oil and deep fry till golden and crisp.
7. Drain on absorbent paper and serve hot with any chutney of your choice.

Papdi Chaat

Ingredients

20 crisp flat *puri*

2 medium potatoes, boiled and thinly sliced

1 large onion, chopped

2-3 tablespoons Date and Tamarind Chutney (page 46)

2 tablespoons Green Chutney (page 12)

1 teaspoon lemon juice

1 teaspoon roasted cumin powder

1 teaspoon *chaat masala*

½ teaspoon rock salt

1 cup *sev*

2 tablespoons pomegranate kernels

2 tablespoons chopped fresh coriander

Method

1. Arrange the *papdi* on a serving dish. Arrange the potatoes neatly on them and sprinkle the chopped onion on top.
2. Drizzle the date and tamarind and green chutneys on each *papdi*.
3. Sprinkle with the lemon juice, roasted cumin powder, *chaat masala* and rock salt.
4. Top with the *sev*, pomegranate and chopped coriander and serve immediately.

Dahi Batata Puri

Ingredients

24 crisp *puri*

1½ cups yogurt, whisked

Salt to taste

1 tablespoon sugar

2 medium potatoes, boiled and chopped

½ cup sprouted beans, blanched

1 teaspoon red chilli powder

½ teaspoon *chaat masala*

¼ cup Green Chutney (page 12)

¼ cup Date and Tamarind Chutney (page 46)

Sev, as required

1 teaspoon roasted cumin powder

2 tablespoons chopped fresh coriander

2 tablespoons pomegranate kernels

Method

1. Add the salt and sugar to the yogurt and whisk till smooth. Place in a refrigerator till ready to use.

2. Mix together the boiled potatoes, sprouted moong, salt, half a teaspoon of chilli powder and *chaat masala*.
3. Make a hole in each *puri*, fill with the potato filling, dip in the yogurt and place on a plate. Alternatively, place the *puri* on the plate and pour the yogurt over, reserving a little for the topping.
4. Put dollops of the green chutney and date and tamarind chutney over the yogurt. Sprinkle the *sev*, remaining chilli powder, roasted cumin powder, chopped coriander and pomegranate kernels over the *puri*, and finally top with the remaining yogurt.
5. Serve immediately.

Green Pea Potli

Ingredients

1½ cups refined flour
Salt to taste
2 tablespoons ghee
Oil for deep-frying

Filling

1 cup shelled green peas, crushed
2 tablespoons oil
1 small onion, peeled and finely chopped
Salt to taste
1 teaspoon red chilli powder
½ teaspoon *garam masala* powder
2 tablespoons fresh coriander, finely chopped
¼ cup grated cheese

Method

1. For the filling, heat two tablespoons of oil in a non-stick pan. Add the onion and sauté over a high heat. When translucent, add the crushed peas and salt. Mix and cook for three to four minutes.

2. Add the chilli powder and *garam masala* powder and mix. Sauté for two minutes and transfer the mixture to a plate. Add the chopped coriander, mix and set aside to cool.

3. Sift the refined flour with the salt. Add the ghee and enough water to make a stiff dough. Divide the dough into twelve equal portions and roll into balls. Flatten each ball slightly and roll out into a small disc.

4. Place the disc in your palm, spread with a little water on the side, place a portion of the filling in the centre. Add the grated cheese. Pleat the edges and gather folds together, twisting slightly to make a *potli*.

5. Heat oil in a non-stick *kadai* and deep-fry the *potli* till golden brown. Drain on absorbent paper and serve hot.

Chilli Cheese Chakri

Ingredients

200 grams cream cheese
4 tortillas
3-4 green chillies
2 fresh red chillies, chopped
½ teaspoon crushed red chillies
Salt to taste
2 tablespoons tomato ketchup
1 medium onion, chopped
2 tablespoons fresh coriander, chopped
A few fresh mint leaves

Method

1. In a bowl, beat the cream cheese with a spoon to a paste. Slit the green chillies, remove seeds, cut into long strips and chop fine.
2. Add the chillies to the cream cheese. Add the chopped fresh red chillies and crushed red chillies; mix well. Add the salt and tomato ketchup. Mix well.
3. Add the chopped onion and coriander and mix once again. Heat a non-stick pan and warm the tortillas on both sides to soften.

4. Spread the warmed tortillas on a flat surface and spread a portion of the chilli-cheese mixture over the tortilla. Roll the tortillas up tightly.
5. Place them in the refrigerator for fifteen minutes.
6. Cut diagonally into small round slices and serve garnished with fresh mint leaves.

Sichuan Chilli Potatoes

Ingredients

4-5 medium potatoes
3 tablespoons corn flour
2 tablespoons oil + to deep-fry
4-5 whole red chillies, broken
8-10 Sichuan peppers, crushed (optional)
1 medium onion, sliced
5-6 cloves garlic, finely chopped
1 teaspoon red chilli paste
1 teaspoon soy sauce
½ teaspoon sugar
Salt to taste
1 tablespoon vinegar
1 stalk spring onion greens, roughly chopped

Method

1. Peel and cut the potatoes into ten to twelve thick wedges.
2. Soak in cold water for half an hour. Heat sufficient water and parboil the potato wedges. Drain and cool.

3. Dust the parboiled potatoes with one and a half tablespoons of corn flour. Heat sufficient oil in a non-stick wok and deep-fry for two minutes or till golden brown and completely cooked and crisp. Drain on absorbent paper. Blend the remaining corn flour in a quarter cup of water.
4. Heat two tablespoons of oil in a non-stick wok, add the broken red chillies and stir-fry for half a minute. Immediately add Sichuan peppers, onion and garlic and continue to stir-fry.
5. Stir in red chilli paste blended with two tablespoons of water, soy sauce, sugar and salt. Stir-fry for half a minute. Add fried potatoes and toss to heat through.
6. Stir in blended corn flour, toss well to mix and add vinegar. Stir-fry for half a minute and serve garnished with spring onion greens.

Paneer Lollies

Ingredients

750 ml (3¾ cups) cow's milk
¼ cup whey, to curdle milk
2½ tablespoons powdered sugar
½ cup grated dark chocolate
¼ tablespoon cocoa butter
¼ cup coloured vermicelli

Method

1. Bring the cow's milk to a boil in a deep pan. Lower heat, add the whey and stir continuously till the milk curdles completely.
2. Strain through a piece of muslin and immediately place the muslin potli on ice to stop the cooking process. Squeeze to remove the excess moisture.
3. Transfer the cottage cheese to a plate and knead with the heel of your hand till smooth. Add the sugar and continue to mash till all the sugar is incorporated.
4. Divide into sixteen equal portions, shape into balls and fix onto toothpicks.

5. Melt the grated chocolate in a microwave-safe bowl in the microwave oven for half a minute; remove and add cocoa butter. Temper the chocolate till it reaches room temperature.
6. Dip the cottage cheese balls in melted chocolate, sprinkle vermicelli generously to cover the balls. Arrange the lollies in a mug and place them in a refrigerator till the chocolate sets.
7. Serve chilled.

Crisp Wontons

Ingredients

24 wonton wrappers

2 tablespoons oil + to deep-fry

4-6 cloves garlic, finely chopped

2 spring onions, finely chopped

2 medium green capsicums, finely chopped

8-10 French beans, finely chopped

2 medium carrots, finely chopped

½ small cabbage, finely chopped

½ teaspoon white pepper powder

Salt to taste

¼ teaspoon MSG (optional)

1 teaspoon light soy sauce

Method

1. Heat two tablespoons of oil in a non-stick wok or pan, add the garlic and stir-fry for half a minute.
2. Add the spring onions, capsicums, French beans, carrots and cabbage and continue to stir-fry for a couple of minutes more, stirring and tossing continuously.

3. Add the white pepper powder, salt, MSG and soy sauce and cook for half a minute. Take the non-stick pan off the heat and allow the vegetables to cool.
4. Divide the prepared filling into twenty-four equal portions. Place a portion of filling in the centre of a wonton wrapper, wet the edges with a little water, fold into half diagonally, twist the ends and press lightly to stick together. Do the same with the rest of the wonton wrappers and filling.
5. Heat sufficient oil in a non-stick wok and deep-fry the wontons for two to three minutes or until crisp and golden brown. Drain on absorbent paper.
6. Serve hot with Sichuan Sauce (page 15).

Patti Samosa

Ingredients

12 *samosa patti*

1 tablespoon oil + for deep-frying

1 teaspoon cumin seeds

1 medium onion, peeled and chopped

1 inch ginger, peeled and grated

3 green chillies, chopped

2 medium potatoes, boiled, peeled and diced

½ cup frozen green peas

Salt to taste

1 teaspoon *chaat masala*

½ teaspoon *garam masala* powder

Method

1. Heat one tablespoon of oil in a non-stick pan; add cumin seeds.
2. When they begin to change colour, add the chopped onion, ginger and green chillies and sauté till the onions turn golden brown. Add the diced potatoes and mix.
3. Mash the peas lightly and add to the potato mixture. Add the salt, *chaat masala*, *garam masala* powder and mix well.

4. Cook for two to three minutes. Transfer to a bowl and mash a little. Set aside to cool. Heat sufficient oil in a non-stick *kadai*.
5. Moisten the surface of each *patti*, with water. Place the filling at one end and fold the *patti* into a triangle. Seal the edges well. Deep-fry in hot oil till golden brown.
6. Drain on absorbent paper and serve hot.

Til Moongphali Aloo

Ingredients

750 grams baby potatoes
1 tablespoon sesame seeds
2 tablespoons peanuts, coarsely crushed
Salt to taste
3 tablespoons oil
1 teaspoon cumin seeds
4 green chillies, chopped
1 inch ginger, chopped
1 tablespoon garlic paste
1 teaspoon roasted cumin powder
1 teaspoon red chilli powder
1½ tablespoons grated fresh coconut
1 teaspoon *garam masala* powder
2 teaspoons lemon juice
2 tablespoons chopped fresh coriander

Method

1. Parboil the unpeeled baby potatoes in salted water and set aside. Press them lightly.
2. Heat the oil in a non-stick *kadai*; add cumin seeds, green chillies and ginger. When the seeds begin to change colour, add the garlic paste and sauté for two or three minutes.

3. Add the potatoes and toss well. Add the sesame seeds, peanuts, roasted cumin powder, chilli powder, coconut and *garam masala* powder. Adjust salt.
4. Continue to cook for five minutes, tossing continuously. Stir in the lemon juice.
5. Serve hot, garnished with chopped coriander.

Tandoori Aloo

Ingredients

16-20 baby potatoes
½ cup yogurt, drained (hung)
Salt to taste
2 teaspoons red chilli paste
1 teaspoon *garam masala* powder
½ teaspoon cumin powder
1 teaspoon white pepper powder
1 tablespoon cashew nut paste
2 teaspoons lemon juice
1 teaspoon dried mango powder
1 tablespoon oil + for basting
1 teaspoon *chaat masala*
1 lemon, cut into wedges

Method

1. Peel and parboil the baby potatoes, prick with a fork and set aside.
2. Make a marinade of the drained yogurt, salt, red chilli paste, *garam masala* powder, cumin powder, white pepper powder, cashew nut paste, lemon juice, dried mango powder and one tablespoon oil.

3 Marinate the potatoes in this mixture for one hour.

4 Preheat a combi-oven to 450°F/230°C/Gas Mark 8.

5 Arrange the marinated potatoes in a single layer in an ovenproof dish and brush with oil.

6 Cook for six minutes. Baste with oil after five minutes and turn the potatoes.

7 Grill TOP for six minutes, brush with oil and turn the potatoes after three minutes.

8 Sprinkle *chaat masala* and serve hot with lemon wedges.

Urulai Chops

Ingredients

6 medium potatoes
Salt to taste
1 teaspoon turmeric powder
20 curry leaves, finely chopped
3 tablespoons rice flour
1½ teaspoons red chilli powder
2 teaspoons coriander powder
2 tablespoons oil + for shallow-frying

Method

1. Peel and slice the potatoes thickly. Parboil in salted water with a pinch of turmeric. Drain.
2. In a bowl, mix the curry leaves, rice flour, red chilli powder, coriander powder, two tablespoons of oil and seven teaspoons of water to a smooth paste.
3. Spread the paste evenly over the potato slices. Set aside for about fifteen minutes.
4. Heat a non-stick *tawa*; add oil and shallow-fry the potato slices over a medium heat for about five minutes till both sides are golden brown. Serve hot.

Stuffed Mushrooms

Ingredients

16 medium fresh button mushrooms

¼ cup crumbled cottage cheese

¼ cup grated processed cheese

1 medium onion, peeled and finely chopped

4-5 cloves garlic, peeled and finely chopped

¼ teaspoon white pepper powder

¼ teaspoon nutmeg powder

Salt to taste

5 tablespoons butter

1 tablespoon lemon juice

Method

1. Remove stalks of mushrooms and chop finely.
2. Place the chopped mushroom stalks, onion, garlic, cottage cheese, processed cheese, white pepper powder, nutmeg powder and salt in a microwave-safe dish.

3. Add two tablespoons of butter and mix well.
4. Cook, uncovered, on HIGH (100%) for six minutes.
5. Stuff the mushroom caps with the mixture; sandwich two caps together, holding them in place with a toothpick.
6. Smear the remaining butter and lemon juice over the mushrooms and cook, uncovered, on MEDIUM (70%) for three minutes. Serve hot.

Chef's Tip: Stuffed Mushrooms taste extra delicious with pepper chilli sauce.

Tikhat Batata

Ingredients

5 large boiled potatoes, cut into 1½-inch cubes

6-8 Kashmiri red chillies

½ tablespoon cumin seeds

½ tablespoon coriander seeds

¼ teaspoon turmeric powder

1 teaspoon dried mango powder

2 tablespoons oil

½ teaspoon mustard seeds

4-5 curry leaves

A pinch of asafoetida

Salt to taste

2 tablespoons chopped fresh coriander

1 tablespoon lemon juice

2 tablespoons Green Chutney (page 12)

2 tablespoons Tamarind Chutney (page 85)

Method

1. Dry-roast the Kashmiri chillies, cumin seeds and coriander seeds for two to three minutes; grind to a coarse paste along with the turmeric powder, dried mango powder and very little water.

2. Heat the oil in a non-stick *kadai*; add the mustard seeds and when they begin to crackle, add the curry leaves.
3. Add the asafoetida and ground *masala* along with half a cup of water and cook over a low heat for two to three minutes, or till the oil separates.
4. Add the potatoes and salt, toss gently, cover and cook over a low heat for two minutes. Stir in the chopped coriander and lemon juice and transfer to a serving bowl.
5. Drizzle the green and tamarind chutneys over the top and serve hot.

TAMARIND CHUTNEY

Soak 1 cup tamarind in two cups of warm water for half an hour. Squeeze out pulp and strain. Cook with 1¼ cups jaggery, and 1 inch cinnamon for fifteen minutes. Stir in 2 tablespoons raisins, salt, ¼ teaspoon black salt, 1 teaspoon red chilli powder, 1 teaspoon roasted cumin powder and 1½ teaspoons dried ginger powder. Cook for a while.

Batter-Fried Onion Rings

Ingredients

6 extra-large onions
2 cups refined flour
3 tablespoons cornflour
Salt to taste
½ teaspoon white pepper powder
½ teaspoon baking powder
½ cup oil + for deep-frying

Method

1. Cut the onions into thick round slices. Separate the onion slices into rings and select only the large outer rings.
2. Sift together the refined flour, cornflour, salt, white pepper powder and baking powder. Gradually stir in half a cup of oil and one-and-a-quarter cups of water to make a thick batter. Whisk the batter continuously for about five to ten minutes.
3. Heat the oil in a non-stick *kadai*. Dip the onion rings in the batter and deep-fry till crisp. Drain on absorbent paper. Serve hot.

Masala Moongphali

Ingredients

1½ cups raw peanuts, unskinned
1 cup gram flour
Salt to taste
¼ teaspoon turmeric powder
1½ teaspoon *chaat masala*
3 teaspoons red chilli powder
A pinch of baking powder
½ teaspoon cumin powder
1 teaspoon *garam masala* powder
2 tablespoons oil + for frying
1 teaspoon *chaat masala*
1 teaspoon red chilli powder

Method

1. Place the peanuts in a large bowl. Add the gram flour, salt, turmeric powder, half a teaspoon of *chaat masala*, two teaspoons of chilli powder, baking powder, cumin powder and *garam masala* powder. Mix well.
2. Sprinkle a little water to moisten the *masala* and coat peanuts well. Add two tablespoons of oil and mix again.

3. Heat sufficient oil in a non-stick *kadai*. When moderately hot, fry a few peanuts at a time till golden brown and crisp. Drain on absorbent paper.
4. Sprinkle the remaining *chaat masala* and red chilli powder. Mix well. Cool and serve immediately; or store in an airtight container.

Note: If the peanuts do not separate easily, add a little more gram flour to the batter.

Corn Patties

Ingredients

¾ cup corn kernels
16 slices of bread
Salt to taste
3-4 green chillies, roughly chopped
2 inches ginger, roughly chopped
1 teaspoon cumin seeds
1 cup milk
¾ cup freshly grated coconut
2 tablespoons fresh coriander, finely chopped
1 tablespoon lemon juice
1 teaspoon sugar
Oil for deep-frying

Method

1. Boil the corn in salted water for eight to ten minutes. Drain.
2. Grind the green chillies and ginger to a coarse paste. Dry-roast the cumin seeds and crush lightly.

3. Cut the bread into rounds using a cutter or the rim of a steel glass. Combine the milk with half a cup of water.
4. In a large bowl, combine the corn kernels, coconut, chopped coriander, green chilli-ginger paste, lemon juice, sugar, crushed cumin seeds and salt and mix well.
5. Dip two slices of bread in the milk; gently squeeze to remove excess liquid. Place a spoonful of corn mixture on one slice, cover with the second slice and press gently to seal the edges.
6. Heat oil in a non-stick *kadai* and deep-fry the *patties* till crisp and golden. Drain on absorbent paper. Serve hot with a chutney of your choice.

Note: Use the remaining edges of bread to make breadcrumbs for later use.

Momos

Ingredients

1 cup refined flour

10 French beans, finely chopped

1 medium carrot, finely chopped

4-5 fresh button mushrooms, finely chopped

2 spring onions, finely chopped

¼ cup bean sprouts

8-10 cashew nuts, chopped

1-inch piece ginger, finely chopped

1 green chilli, finely chopped

8-10 black peppercorns, crushed

½ tablespoon light soy sauce

1 teaspoon sesame oil

¼ teaspoon MSG (optional)

Salt to taste

1 spring onion green, chopped

Method

1. Mix the refined flour with five tablespoons of water and knead into a stiff dough. Cover with a damp cloth and set aside for fifteen minutes.

2. For the filling, in a large bowl, combine the French beans, carrot, mushrooms, spring onions, bean sprouts, cashew nuts, ginger, green chilli, peppercorns, soy sauce, sesame oil, MSG and salt to taste.
3. Divide the dough into sixteen equal portions and roll into small thin discs.
4. Place a spoonful of the vegetable filling in the centre of each disc and bring the sides together in the centre, pinching firmly together to form a dumpling.
5. Line a steamer rack with a clean, damp piece of muslin and arrange the momos on it. Place the rack in the steamer, cover and steam for eight to ten minutes, until the momos are cooked through.
6. Transfer to a serving plate. Garnish with spring onion greens and serve hot with Sichuan Sauce (page 15).

GLOSSARY

English	Hindi	English	Hindi
Asafoetida	Hing	Coriander seeds	Sabut dhania
Banana, unripe	Kachcha kela	Coriander, fresh	Dhania patti
Bay leaf	Tej patta	Corn kernels	Makai ke dane
Beans, sprouted	Ankurit moong	Cottage cheese	Paneer
Butter	Makkhan	Cream	Malai
Cabbage	Patta gobhi	Cumin seeds	Jeera
Capsicum	Shimla mirch	Curry leaves	Kadi patta
Carom seeds	Ajwain	Dates	Khajoor
Carrot	Gajar	Fennel seeds	Badi saunf
Cashew nuts	Kaju	Fenugreek leaves, dried	Kasuri methi
Cauliflower	Phool gobhi	Fenugreek seeds	Methi dana
Chickpeas	Kabuli chana	French beans	Farsi
Cloves	Laung	Garlic	Lehsun
Coconut, dried	Khopra	Ginger, dried	Saunth
Coconut, fresh	Nariyal	Gram flour	Besan

English	Hindi
Gram, Bengal split	Chana dal
Gram, bengal split roasted	Daalia
Gram, black skinless split	Dhuli urad dal
Gram, green skinless split	Moong dal
Honey	Shahad
Jaggery	Gur
Mango, dried and powdered	Amchur
Mint	Pudina
Mushrooms	Khumb/dhingri
Mustard	Rai/sarson
Nutmeg	Jaiphal
Onion seeds	Kalonji
Peanuts	Moongphalli
Peas, green	Matar

English	Hindi
Peas, yellow dried	Safed matar
Peppercorns, black	Kali mirch
Peppercorns, white	Safed mirch
Pigeon peas, split	Tuvar dal/arhar dal
Pomegranate kernels	Anar ke dane
Poppy seeds	Khuskhus
Raisins	Kishmish
Refined flour	Maida
Rice, parboiled	Ukda chawal
Sesame seeds	Til
Spinach	Palak
Spring onion	Hare pyaaz
Spring onion greens	Hare pyaaz ke patte
Tamarind	Imli
Turmeric	Haldi
Vinegar	Sirka
Yogurt	Dahi